MORE GLASS
PAINTING
DESIGNS

More Glass
Painting
Designs

JANET EADIE

Kangaroo Press

MORE GLASS PAINTING DESIGNS
First published in Australia in 2002 by Kangaroo Press
An imprint of Simon & Schuster (Australia) Pty Limited
20 Barcoo Street, East Roseville NSW 2069

A Viacom Company
Sydney New York London

Cataloguing-in-Publication data:

Eadie, Janet.
More glass painting designs

ISBN 0 7318 1149 6.

CIP TO COME

Cover and internal design by Anna Soo Design
Illustrations by Janet Eadie
Photographs by Steve Palin
Typeset in 11/16pt Sabon
Printed through Colorcraft Ltd., Hong Kong

10 9 8 7 6 5 4 3 2 1

ACKNOWLEDGMENTS

I would like to thank all of you who showed such enthusiasm for my first glass painting book. This has certainly encouraged me to create another collection of designs. I hope that you enjoy this one just as much. So thank you to my publishers, Simon & Schuster, for recognising the interest and suggesting I put together a second book on glass painting designs.

Thank you also to my family for their helpful hints and patience while my creations were found drying in nearly every room of the house!

A sincere thank you to Steve Palin, for his wonderful photography which is featured throughout this book and for first introducing me to glass painting.

Thank you to Birch Haberdashery for supplying me with the Gallery Glass Window Colour used on the projects in this book.

CONTENTS

The Projects

INTRODUCTION

I have been working with glass paint for around nine years and still get a lot of pleasure from the combination of vibrant colours, and the fact that the simpler the design, the more effective the end result will be.

My first experience of glass painting was to demonstrate the use of this medium at retail stores and I soon realised how popular it is. Once people were shown how easy it was, they quickly became enthusiastic about this great pastime. Very little equipment is needed apart from leading, paint and glass. No wonder it is a popular craft.

I have tried to pass on to you the easiest methods and helpful hints that I have discovered in the years of using the glass paint. My designs in this book are presented as either framed art or 'peel and press' designs, but could be adapted for use on windows or doors in your home.

Since my first book, there have been some exciting new colours introduced to the Plaid range of Gallery Glass Window Colour paint, which I have enjoyed incorporating into my designs.

Add this book to your collection, and have fun creating more glass painted projects for your home.

EQUIPMENT

The basic materials list is fairly simple and you will already have many of these around your home.

You will need:

- A tube of Liquid Leading.
- A selection of glass paints.
- Tracing paper to transfer the designs from book.
- Pen-Use a dark pen to trace out your design.
- Toothpicks to help spread the paint to the edge of leaded outline.
- A pin to prick any air bubbles, should they occur.
- Skewer – A metal skewer can be used to pierce a hole in top of leading nozzle.
- Paper towels to wipe off excess paint from nozzle.
- Cotton buds – used to wipe away any excess paint if errors occur in applying it.
- Plastic A4 sleeves to work the designs onto, prior to drying and peeling off plastic.
- Scissors, which can be used to snip away, any mistakes in the dried leading.
- Scalpel or craft knife – if it is necessary to remove any damaged area of dried paint, a scalpel can be used to cut alongside the leading and peel away the unwanted paint film.
- Sharpened eraser, which glides along glass or plastic surface, to remove any mistakes in the wet leaded outline.
- Sticky tape – Some designs call for very fine leading detail. By snipping off the tip of nozzle, you can wind sticky tape on an angle around existing nozzle to create a much finer tip.
- Varnish – Only necessary to use over the dried, cured paint to protect items like storage jars if they are to be washed in water. Make sure you do a test first to check the compatibility of varnish to paint.
- Frames – make sure the frames you purchase have the 'clip-in' glass so that the glass can be easily removed for painting then reinserted into frame.

COLOUR CONVERSION CHART

You may wish to substitute another type of glass paint. The list below is a general guide for conversion of colours.

Plaid Gallery Glass	DecoArt Rainbow	Plaid Gallery Glass	Deco Art Rainbow
Snow White	Snowflake White	Amethyst	Lively Lavender
Crystal Clear	Raindrop	Purple	Great Grape
White Pearl	White Pearl	Celadon Green	–
Cameo Ivory	White Chocolate	Lime Green	Lemon Lime
Clear Frost	Crystal Glitter	Emerald Green	–
Silver Sparkle	Silver Pearl	Kelly Green	Leaf Green
Gold Sparkle	Gold Pearl	Ivy Green	Dark Green
Copper Sparkle	–	Turquoise	Tropical Turquoise
Champagne	–	Royal Blue	Primary Blue
Light Brown	Root Beer Brown	Blue Diamond	Blue Cloud
Cocoa Brown	–	Blue Sparkle	–
Amber	–	Sapphire	–
Canyon Coral	Pastel Peach	Denim Blue	–
Orange Poppy	Orange Lollipop	Slate Blue	–
Citrus Yellow	–	Charcoal	Grey
Sunny Yellow	Primary Yellow	Black Onyx	–
Ruby Red	Christmas Red	Glow in the dark Blue	–
Rose Quartz	–	Glow in the dark Yellow	Glow in the dark
Hot Pink	Tickled Pink	Glow in the dark Green	–
Berry Red	Burgundy Blast	Glow in the dark Orange	–
Magenta Royale	Fuchsia	Glow in the dark Red	–

TECHNIQUES

Preparation of Glass Surface

Before painting, the glass surface must be extremely clean to allow for paint adhesion. The best method is to use a soft cloth rinsed out in hot soapy water to clean the glass, and a second soft cloth to polish it dry.

Avoid leaving any chemical cleaners on the glass, as they may interfere with the paint.

If the design is to be worked onto an existing window or door, you will need to attach the design behind the glass. Remember to work the design on the inside of your home, as the paint is not to be exposed to harsh weather conditions. You should also allow for a certain amount of airflow next to the paint, so that moisture is not left for any length of time on the paint in wet or humid conditions.

Preparing Liquid Leading Bottle

Liquid Leading is a non-toxic outline paint that comes in three sizes (2 oz, 4 oz and 8 oz). You will need to remove the cap and pierce a hole in the tip of nozzle with a metal skewer.

Alternatively, you can use scissors to snip a very small portion off the nozzle and wind sticky tape on an angle to recreate another nozzle. This is beneficial if you want to create a thin stream of leading for fine outline detail.

When a thicker leaded outline is required for a large scale project, you will need to simply snip off a portion from nozzle to achieve the required width of leading.

Throughout your outlining work, always remember to shake the contents of bottle to the tip, to avoid the leading from spattering when it becomes almost empty.

Outlining the Design

Place the design underneath the glass or inside A4 plastic sleeve. Shake the contents of the bottle down to the nozzle tip. Start the leading outline by first squeezing the bottle, and as the leading begins to flow, hold the bottle about five mm above the work surface. Move your hand slowly and steadily, following the design outline. This will allow the leading to 'drape' over the outline, rather than being squashed with the nozzle if it is held firmly to the surface.

It would be difficult to complete the leading in one continuous outline. So throughout your work, stop the flow of leading by not squeezing the bottle, but by touching the nozzle tip momentarily onto the work surface. This will allow you to turn your work in a more convenient position and commence the next line of the design. Joins can be smoothed over with a pin while the leading is still wet.

Mistakes in leading outline can be removed by either two ways:

1. The easiest way for larger areas is to allow the leading to dry (approximately 12 to 24 hours) and use scissors to snip the damaged

leading away. Re-pipe, and smooth any joins with a pin.

2. Minor errors in uneven leading can be removed while leading is still wet by using the edge of a sharpened eraser. Glide the edge of eraser next to the edge of leading, removing any excess width in wet leading.

Mixing Paint Colours

There are three options for mixing colours:

1. The complete nozzle on paint tube can be removed and colours can be mixed within each bottle. Remember to stir well with a skewer to combine colour, rather than shaking vigorously which could cause excessive air-bubbles. This method is necessary when large areas of a mixed colour are required.

2. Small amounts of colour can be mixed on a clean tile or plastic plate. Combine well with a palette knife, and then scoop up with palette knife and place in required area of your design.

3. Colours can also be mixed within the dried leading outline. Squeeze a puddle of each colour straight onto project and combine well with a toothpick to create a new colour. Spread paint to meet edge of leading and comb through with a toothpick. For a 'streaky' effect, you can squeeze individual colour directly onto your design, then using toothpick in a back and forth motion, you can streak the colours together, until it becomes slightly merged, where both colours join.

Note: to soften the shade of a colour, you can add Crystal Clear or one of the lighter colours such as Snow White or White Pearl to existing colours.

Fabric Paint Detail

Fabric paint can be used over the top of the dry glass paint to give more noticeable, solid detail, because it remains opaque. The dimensional paint can also be applied in a finer stream, so it is very useful for areas where this is required (for example, fine face details, stamens on flowers, etc). Just allow the glass paint to cure for 24 hours before adding fabric paint over the top.

Some of the Glitter fabric paint can be a very effective addition to your artwork. They come in a range of colours and will make your projects look very creative if used on butterfly wings, the scales on fish, fairy designs or to highlight certain areas of your designs.

Cleaning

Allow your glass paint to cure for at least a week before attempting to clean the surface. Always use a soft cloth, rung out in hot soapy water to clean the paint surface, then wipe dry with another soft cloth.

Do not use excessive water on your glass paint, or solvent-based cleaners or abrasive cloths.

Varnishing

I would only recommend the use of varnish over the top of glass paint where the decorated item will be exposed to very moist conditions, such as in a steamy bathroom or on items such as decorated jars, which may need to be washed after use.

You will first need to do a test to be sure the varnish you use is compatible with the glass paint.

Allow the glass paint to cure for approximately one week before applying varnish over the top of the painted area.

If you use a spray varnish you may need to mask off around the painted area. A liquid varnish will need to be painted slightly outside the glass paint to provide protection from moisture.

Hints

Leading outline

Upon starting this craft, most people are concerned with their leaded outline being uneven. With practice this soon becomes smoother, but I have found the easiest way to achieve the best result is to:

Begin by squeezing the tube of leading with the nozzle close to the work surface. Once the flow of leading has started, hold the tube approximately five mm above the surface and move in a slow, even pace, which will allow the leading to drape in a line over the design outline. When you need to stop the flow of leading (preferably at a point where the design lines intersect) stop squeezing the tube and lightly touch the nozzle onto the work surface, which will stop the flow. At this point you can turn your work around for a more comfortable position and commence the next line of your design. Any enlarged joins of leading can usually be smoothed with the point of a pin in wet leading.

Very fine leading detail

Sometimes finer detail is required in some designs (such as the faces on fairies or the eyes/mouth on the bears and cats). I have found the easiest way to achieve this is to pull the wet leading into shape with the tip of a pin.

For example, for a finer mouth, squeeze a small dot of leading, and use a pin to pull into fine points at either side. A sharper point can also be achieved at the end of a line by using a pin to pull it into shape.

You can also make a much finer nozzle on the end of leading tube by snipping away a small portion of nozzle and then use a 5cm length of sticky tape to wind around the end of the nozzle. Position it at an acute angle at first, before winding it around the nozzle. The sharper the angle the tape is first placed, then the finer the nozzle will be.

Uneven flow of leading

This is usually due to a slight blockage in the nozzle. Make sure you frequently wipe the nozzle onto a paper towel, when piping the outline of the design. If leading is allowed to dry on the end of nozzle, it will hamper the flow. You may need to unscrew the cap and use a skewer to push out any lumps of dried leading.

Remember to shake the contents down to the tip of nozzle frequently throughout your piping, especially if working with a semi-empty tube. If you don't, pockets of air will be caught within the leading tube and could cause the leading to spatter.

Uneven appearance of dry Window Colour

When applying the Window Colour, it is difficult to judge how thick or how even the application is. This is due to the paint being opaque at this stage and when it dries it will sometimes appear deeper or more transparent in areas. Unless the paint is 'combed' through with a toothpick when wet, it will dry deeper in colour where there is more paint thickness.

A more even colour will be achieved by combing through the wet paint in a back and forth motion. Sometimes I will comb through in first one direction, then turn my work and comb through in another direction which will even up the level of paint in each outlined section. The exception to this, however, is when using Crystal Clear as a background paint when a deliberate texture can be created by swirling through in either circles or a figure '8' motion.

Light holes in dry paintwork

Once your work has dried and is positioned with light shining through, it will be more obvious where you may have missed pushing the paint to meet the edge of the leading. All that is needed is to pick up a small amount of paint on the end of a toothpick and touch onto the missed area. It will then dry with a more uniform appearance.

Cloudy Crystal Clear paint

If you are working with the paint on days with high moisture content in the air, some of the moisture may become trapped between the glass and the paint. This will leave the Crystal Clear paint with a slightly cloudy appearance. It may also occur if the Crystal Clear paint is applied very thickly in some areas.

Removing damaged areas

If it is necessary to remove parts of your work once the paint has dried, you can use a craft knife to cut as close to the leading on all sides of the damaged section. The paint can then be lifted away in a complete film and a new application can be applied. Just remember not to cut too firmly with a sharp scalpel, or the glass will be scored if you intend removing the entire painting in the future.

Paint running off a curved or vertical surface

The Gallery Glass Window Colour has been designed for use on either a flat, curved or vertical surface. However, if working on a surface other than a horizontal one, you will need to ease up on the amount of paint being applied.

Many people ask me how much to apply? This is quite easy to determine:

Too little paint applied will not be enough to spread out to meet the edge of leading.

Too much paint applied to a vertical or curved surface will need to go somewhere and it will start to run off the edge. Leave approximately 10–15 mm ($\frac{1}{4}$–$\frac{1}{2}$ in) clear space from the bottom line of leading in any section of a vertical design. You can then push the paint to meet the edge of the leading. Any further drop of paint can then be accommodated within this area.

DESIGN APPLICATION

Direct Application

In this book I have worked the designs directly onto either glass jars, framed glass or I have worked the designs onto plastic to be used as 'peel and press' designs when dry. This is known as **Direct Application** of the paint onto the work surface.

The project is laid flat while the leading outline is piped directly onto the surface. When the leading is dry, the design is coloured in with glass paint to complete the project. This is by far the easiest method, but for decorating glass in existing doors and windows, you will need to use the **Vertical Application** discussed in the next section.

For Direction Application you will need to lay the project down flat on a suitable workbench and attach the design behind the glass or plastic. The coffee jars can also be worked directly onto by holding the design in place inside the jars with scrunched up plastic shopping bags and carefully piping onto the curved surface.

Leading Use Liquid Leading to outline the design, following the instructions on page 6. When the leading outline is complete, you will need to set it aside to dry for approximately 12 to 24 hours or until dry to touch.

Window Colour paints This paint will dry slightly deeper in colour than it appears in the bottle. The colour on the bottle label is more indicative of the final colour.

Each outlined section should be coloured in and combed through to complete before moving to the next section. This means to first apply the paint and then comb through with the pointed end of a toothpick to smooth out the surface area.

To do this you will need to squeeze the paint into the outlined section until enough paint has been applied for you to spread evenly to meet the edge the leading. Make sure the paint touches the leading on all edges, as this seals the leading onto the glass. If you have missed doing this in some places, it can always be touched up with more paint at a later stage (refer to Hints section on page 7).

The next step is to 'comb' through the paint with a toothpick, which will make the paint distribution more even. Consequently when the paint dries the colour will be more uniform. Move the toothpick in a back and forth motion similar to sketching.

At this stage the paint application may look a little messy because the paint will be opaque and more noticeable where it has gone slightly over some of the leading. When the paint dries to a transparent finish it will reveal all of the leading outline.

If there are any larger air bubbles, use a pin to burst these. Generally the very fine bubbles that sometimes occur can be left. Some bubbles are quite persistent, so within a time span of about 20 minutes, try to burst these. After that time a skin will begin to form on the paint as it sets.

Background A very effective textured background can be achieved by using Crystal Clear Window Colour. Spread the paint to meet all edges of the leading, then wait five to ten minutes before using the nozzle or a toothpick to swirl through the paint. This will create a slightly mottled, textured appearance when the paint dries to a clear finish.

Alternatively, a background can be applied with a brush. By doing this the paint will be applied very thinly, so with this method it is best to use Clear Frost Window Colour if a clear background is required. Squeeze some paint onto a tile or plastic plate, and apply in a criss-cross fashion to the background area using a 12 mm (½ inch) flat brush. Apply the paint slightly over the edge of all leading area. Because this brush technique applies the paint in a very thin layer, it will not be noticeable if some of the existing design is painted onto. This is necessary so all areas of glass are sealed, which in turn protects the design from moisture getting underneath and perhaps eventually causing the paint to lift off.

For a smooth background colour, you will need to apply the paint and spread it to meet all leading edges. Next, comb through with a toothpick to create uniform colour.

Once all the paintwork has been completed, leave the project lying flat for 24 to 48 hours while drying. The drying time will be dependent on the amount of humidity in the air.

If creating the 'peel and press' designs, they can then be peeled away from the plastic backing at this stage, and attached to a clean glass surface.

Vertical Application

The designs in this book can be adapted to use on doors and windows within your home. Because the glass will be in a vertical position, you will have to use a combination approach for applying the design. The design should be worked on the inside of your home so the paint is not exposed to the elements.

You will first need to prepare sections of your design onto plastic A4 sleeves. These are then treated as any other 'peel and press' design (refer to method at bottom of page). Plus you will need to prepare some pre-piped leading strips to connect these design elements to complete the design on your existing window or door.

Both 'peel and press' designs and the leading strips are self-adhering onto a clean glass surface, providing all the air is pushed out from underneath. They can be re-positioned if necessary.

Method

Paper Design
Firstly, attach the paper design behind the glass on your window or door. You may need to enlarge or reduce the design on a photocopier to achieve the correct size. This will then guide you as to exactly where to press the 'peel and press' areas of the design.

Peel and Press method
Peel the design elements off the plastic A4 sleeves and press firmly onto the glass. Use your fingertips to press out any trapped air.

Leading strips

You will also need to prepare some lengths of leading strips, which will be used to connect the design. The leading strips can also be piped onto the plastic A4 sleeves and allowed to dry for 12 to 24 hours. Once dry, they will peel off the plastic (snip off any thicker ends), then press into place. As you apply the strips, use your fingernail to press an indent at the exact point you need to cut with scissors. When positioning the leading strips, be careful not to stretch them too much.

DO NOT overlap any of the leading strips, as they will not attach permanently onto the glass surface.

If you have cut some of the leading lines too short, you can apply a dot of leading straight from the tube to complete the line. It is a good idea to squeeze a dot of leading over all the joins to completely seal the outline.

Background

The third and final stage of completing your vertical design is to apply the background paint.

This can be applied directly from the bottle to the vertical glass. Start at the upper corner of your design and work in sections. Run the nozzle backwards and forwards, making sure the paint touches all areas of the leading.

Remember to use less paint at the bottom of each section to allow for a slight 'drop' as the paint dries. If the paint starts to run over the bottom line of leading, you will need to ease back on the amount of paint being applied approximately 10 to 15 mm (¼ to ½ in) from the lower edge. Then just push the existing paint with a toothpick to meet the lower edge.

If a Crystal Clear textured background is being applied, you will need to apply the paint and then wait 5-10 minutes, before using the nozzle or a toothpick to swirl through the paint to create a textured effect.

If painting on the background with a 12 mm (½ in) flat brush with Clear Frost, follow the same instructions as described under Direct Application. This is a very quick method for covering a large background area and will use less paint.

For a smooth background finish, you will need to apply the paint, making sure it meets all edges of the leading. Next, comb through the wet paint with a toothpick, to make the colour more uniform. This will only be noticeable when it dries.

THE PROJECTS

COFFEE JARS

The coffee jar designs are forever popular, so here is a selection of themes and colourways for you to use on those jars stored at the back of your cupboard. They will certainly brighten up any kitchen shelf.

First, be sure to thoroughly clean the jars, and soak off any remaining labels. You may find some eucalyptus oil will remove any label residue, which won't soak off in hot soapy water.

Once jars are clean, dry well, and trace off the designs onto greaseproof paper. Insert the design inside the jar and fill out the inside of the jar with crumpled plastic grocery bags. This will help hold the paper design firmly to the inside surface of the jar.

*As an option, you can create the designs on A4 plastic sleeves and when dry, peel off plastic and then adhere the designs to the jars.

Lay the jar on its side, and hold steady with a book either side. Now you can begin to pipe the design outline in leading. Once leading is dry, colour in with Window Colour, following the directions for individual design.

If you intend washing the jars, by immersing in water after decorating, you will need to protect the glass paint with varnish. Allow the paint to cure for one week before painting with a compatible varnish such as Cabot's Crystal Clear. Use a soft bristled brush to paint the varnish over the glass paint, slightly outside the outer edges of the design. This will protect your paint from moisture. You could also use a spray varnish, but do a test first; to be sure it is compatible with your glass paint.

DO NOT leave painted jars soaking in water, or wash in a dishwasher. It is best just to wipe over the painted surface with a soft cloth, wrung out in hot soapy water.

HEARTS

Illustrated in Figure 8
MATERIALS

Large Moccona coffee jar
Plaid Gallery Glass Liquid Leading:
  Soft Black
Plaid Gallery Glass Window Colour:
  Snow White
  Hot Pink
  Ruby Red
  Magenta Royale
  Berry Red

3 or 4 plastic grocery bags
toothpick
pin
greaseproof paper
water-based varnish (eg. Cabots Crystal Clear)
brush, 12mm (½ in) flat

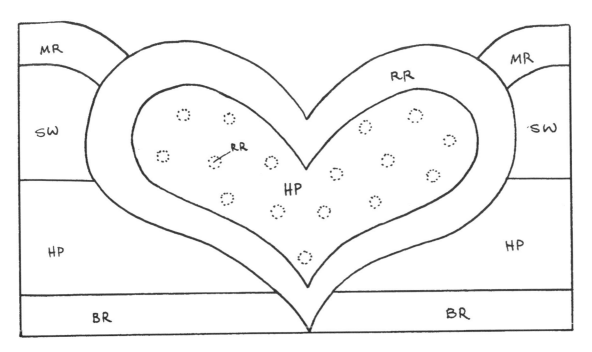

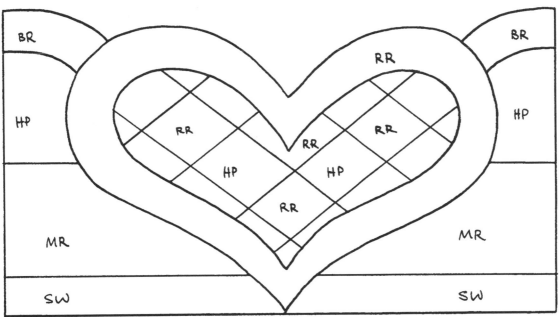

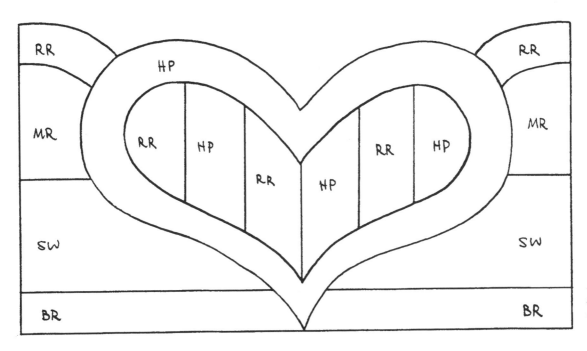

Illustration shown at 90% of original size

METHOD

Trace the design onto greaseproof paper and cut out to fit inside jar. Pad inside of jar with plastic bags to hold design firmly in place for inside glass surface.

Lay jar flat to pipe the design in Liquid Leading. Allow leading to dry for approximately 12 to 24 hours.

Apply Window Colour, referring to the design for colour placement.

Comb through the paint in each section with a toothpick, to distribute the paint evenly.

Use a pin to burst any larger air bubbles and then allow the paint to dry for 24 hours, before sitting jars upright.

Spotted Heart Apply a base colour of Hot Pink first and comb through to distribute the paint evenly. Allow the Hot Pink paint to dry before squeezing Ruby Red spots over the base colour.

FISH

Illustrated in Figure 10

MATERIALS

Large Moccona coffee jar
Plaid Gallery Glass Liquid Leading
  Soft Black
Plaid Gallery Glass Window Colour:
  Blue Diamond
  Royal Blue
  Turquoise
  Lime Green
  Kelly Green
  Emerald Green
3 or 4 plastic grocery bags
toothpick
pin
greaseproof paper
water-based varnish (eg. Cabot's Crystal
  Clear)
brush, 12mm (½ in) flat

METHOD

Trace the design onto greaseproof paper and cut out to fit inside jar. Pad inside of jar with plastic bags to hold design firmly in place on inside of glass surface.

Lay jar flat to pipe the design in Liquid Leading. Allow leading to dry for approximately 12 to 24 hours.

Apply Window Colour, referring to the design for colour placement.

Comb through the paint in each section with a toothpick, to distribute the paint evenly.

Use a pin to burst any larger air bubbles and then allow the paint to dry for 24 hours, before sitting jars upright.

Spotted Fish Apply Lime Green to the fish body and comb through paint with a toothpick to distribute paint. Allow paint to dry, before squeezing Turquoise spots over the base colour and then in the centre of Turquoise spots, squeeze smaller dots of Lime Green.

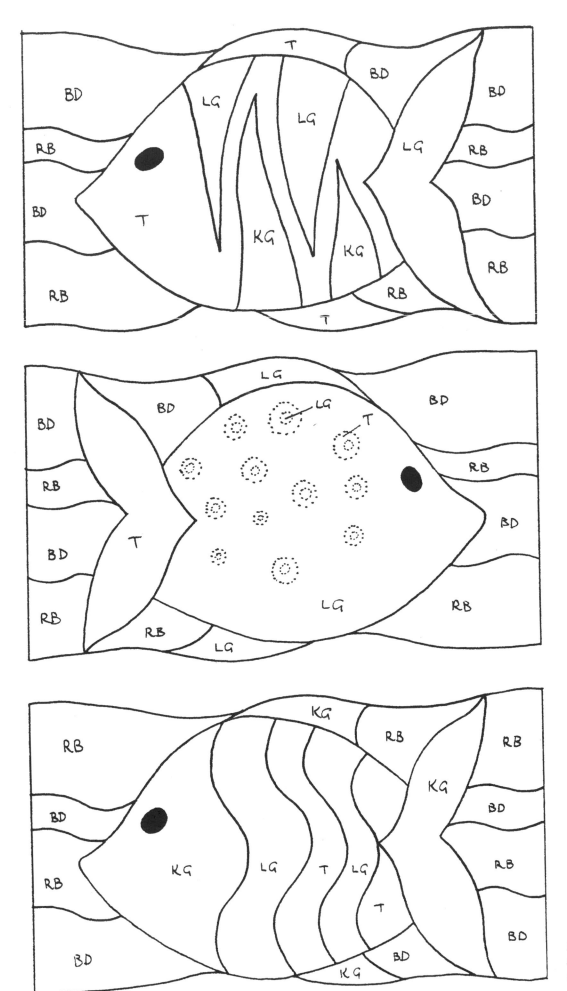

Illustration shown at 90% of original size

BUTTERFLIES

Illustrated in Figure 11

MATERIALS

Large Moccona coffee jar

Plaid Gallery Glass Liquid Leading:
 Soft Black

Plaid Gallery Glass Window Colour:
 Crystal Clear
 White Pearl
 Magenta Royale
 Amethyst
 Purple
 Denim Blue
 Sapphire

three or four plastic grocery bags

toothpick

pin

greaseproof paper

water-based varnish (eg. Cabot's Crystal
 Clear)

brush, 12mm (½ in) flat

METHOD

Trace the design onto greaseproof paper and cut out to fit inside jar. Pad inside of jar with plastic bags to hold design firmly in place on inside of glass surface.

Lay jar flat to pipe the design in Liquid Leading. Allow leading to dry approximately 12 to 24 hours.

Apply Window Colour, referring to the design for colour placement.

Comb through the paint in each section with a toothpick, to distribute the paint evenly.

Use a pin to burst any larger air bubbles and then allow the paint to dry for 24 hours, before sitting jars upright.

Illustration shown at 90% of original size

FRAMED GLASS ART
TULIPS IN POT

Illustrated in Figure 12

MATERIALS

Frame with clip-in glass approximately 30 x 40.5 cm (11 ¾ x 16 in)

Plaid Gallery Glass Liquid Leading:

  Soft Black

Plaid Gallery Glass Window Colour:

  Crystal Clear

  Magenta Royale

  Hot Pink

  Kelly Green

  Emerald Green

  Snow White

  Sapphire Blue

  Denim Blue

Toothpicks

Pin

METHOD

Remove glass from frame to decorate and place design underneath.

Use Liquid Leading to outline the design and set aside to dry for approximately 12 to 24 hours.

Refer to design for colour placement. Work each outlined section individually, and apply Window Colour in the following sequence:

Tulips Apply Magenta Royale to the base of tulip and Hot Pink in the upper portion. Comb through the individual colours to distribute evenly, then while both paints are still wet, use the tip of toothpick in a back and forth motion to streak the two colours together. Complete one flower at a time before moving on to the next.

Leaves Refer to design for correct leaf colour to use and apply either Kelly Green, or Emerald Green. Comb through the wet paint with a toothpick to distribute colour more evenly.

Pot Use White Pearl to paint the pot. Because White Pearl remains slightly opaque when it dries, it is especially important to comb evenly through the wet paint as the combing will remain visible when the paint has dried.

Tablecloth Alternate between Sapphire Blue and Denim Blue to paint the stripes in this area. Comb through to distribute the paint.

Background Apply Crystal Clear to the background areas. First apply the paint, making sure the paint touches the edge of leading. Wait approximately five minutes before using a toothpick to swirl through the wet paint. This will create an interesting, slightly mottled texture when the paint dries.

Burst any significant air bubbles with a pin and leave your work to dry in a horizontal position for 24 to 48 hours.

Paint frame in a coordinating colour, and when dry, clip glass back into frame.

Illustration shown at 65% of original size

CINERARIAS IN POT

Illustrated in Figure 13

MATERIALS

Frame with clip-in glass approximately 30 x
  40.5 cm
  (11 ¾ x 16 in)
Plaid Gallery Glass Liquid Leading:
  Soft Black
Plaid Gallery Glass Window Colour:
  Crystal Clear
  Sapphire Blue
  Denim Blue
  Ivy Green
  Kelly Green
  White Pearl
  Sunny Yellow
Toothpicks
Pin

METHOD

Remove glass from frame to decorate and
place design underneath.

Use Liquid Leading to outline the design
and set aside to dry for approximately 12 to
24 hours.

Refer to design for colour placement. Work
each outlined section individually and apply
Window Colour in the following sequence:

Cinerarias Paint the majority of the petal with
Sapphire Blue, leaving a small area at the
centre. To this area, apply White Pearl and
while both paints are still wet, use a toothpick
to streak the colours together.

Use Sunny Yellow to paint the centre of each
flower. I left the paint to set for about ten
minutes, before using the broad end of a
toothpick to pad up and down, giving a
slightly mottled texture to the centres.

Leaves Refer to design for correct leaf colour
to use and apply either Kelly Green, or Ivy
Green. Comb through the wet paint with a
toothpick to distribute the colour more evenly.

Pot Use Denim Blue to paint the pot. Comb
through the wet paint with a toothpick to
make colour distribution more even.

Tablecloth Alternate between White Pearl and
Sunny Yellow to paint the stripes in this area.
Comb through to distribute the paint.

Background Apply Crystal Clear to the
background areas. First apply the paint,
making sure the paint touches the edge of the
leading. Wait approximately five minutes
before using a toothpick to swirl through the
wet paint. This will create an interesting,
slightly mottled texture when the paint dries.

Burst any significant air bubbles with a pin
and leave your work to dry in a horizontal
position for 24 to 48 hours.

Paint frame in a coordinating colour, and
when dry, clip glass back into frame.

Illustration shown at 65% of original size

PEACOCK

Illustrated in Figure 14
MATERIALS

Frame with clip-in glass, approximately 34 x
  27 cm (13 ½ x 10 ½ in)
Plaid Gallery Glass Liquid Leading:
  Soft Black
Plaid Gallery Glass Window Colour:
  Crystal Clear
  Amber
  Blue Diamond
  Royal Blue
  Sapphire
  Lime Green
  Emerald Green
  Turquoise
Plaid Dimensional Fabric Paint:
  Blue Ocean Glitter
Toothpicks
Pin

METHOD

Remove glass from frame to decorate and place design underneath.

Use Liquid Leading to outline the design and set aside to dry for approximately 12 to 24 hours.

Refer to design for colour placement. Work each outlined section individually, and apply Window Colour in the following sequence:

Peacock Body Apply Turquoise to the head, down to the middle of body. Then apply Royal Blue to the remainder of body. Comb through each colour individually, before using the toothpick in a back and forth motion to combine the colours slightly where they join.
Legs/Feet Use Amber to colour this area and comb through with a toothpick to distribute the paint evenly.

Tail Complete each section at a time – apply Lime Green to the base of tail. Use Emerald Green in the middle of this section and at the tip of tail use Turquoise to colour. Comb each paint section separately before using toothpick in a back and forth motion to combine colours where they meet.

Circle Features Apply Lime Green to the outer area of each circle and Royal Blue to the inner area. Comb through paint to even out the colour.

Background Apply Crystal clear to the background area. First apply the paint, making sure the paint touches the edge of the leading. Wait approximately five minutes before using a toothpick to swirl through the wet paint. This will create an interesting, slightly mottled texture when the Crystal Clear paint dries.

Border At each corner, use Royal Blue to colour each square. Paint the inside area of the border strip with Sapphire and the outer area with Blue Diamond. Comb through the paint to distribute evenly.

Burst any significant air-bubbles with a pin and leave your work in a horizontal position for 24–48 hours.

Peacock Crown When all Window Colour paint has dried, use the Blue Ocean Glitter dimensional paint to squeeze 3 large dots to form the crown. This adds a nice contrast over the top of the glass paint.

Paint frame in coordinating colour and when dry, clip glass back into frame.

Illustration shown at 70% of original size

BEAR ON SWING

Illustrated in Figure 15

MATERIALS

Frame with clip-in glass approximately
  21.5 x 25 cm (8 ½ x 9 ¾ in)
Plaid Gallery Glass Liquid Leading:
  Soft Black
Plaid Gallery Glass Window Colour:
  Crystal Clear
  Cameo Ivory
  Sunny Yellow
  Amber
  Lime Green
  Emerald Green
  Turquoise
Toothpicks
Pin

METHOD

Remove glass from frame to decorate and place design underneath.

Use Liquid Leading to outline the design and set aside to dry for approximately 12 to 24 hours.

When piping the mouth in leading, use a pin to pull the wet leading to a finer line.

Refer to design for colour placement. Work each outlined section individually, and apply Window Colour in the following sequence:

Bear Use Amber to colour all parts of the bear. Comb through paint with a toothpick to distribute the paint colour evenly.

Use Cameo Ivory for the nose section and feet.

Rope and Swing Paint with Sunny Yellow.

Leaves Use various greens (refer to design details) to colour the leaves.

Grass Use Emerald Green to paint the area of grass at the base of picture. Comb through wet paint to distribute evenly.

Background Apply Crystal Clear to the background areas. First apply the paint, making sure the paint touches the edge of leading. Wait approximately five minutes before using a toothpick to swirl through the wet paint. This will create the interesting, slightly mottled texture when the paint dries.

Burst any significant air bubbles with a pin and leave your work to dry in a horizontal position for 24 to 48 hours.

Paint frame in a coordinating colour, and when dry, clip glass back into frame.

Illustration shown at actual size

BIKINI BEAR

Illustrated in Figure 16

MATERIALS

Frame with clip-in glass approximately
  21.5 x 25 cm (8 ½ x 9 ¾ in)
Plaid Gallery Glass Liquid Leading:
  Soft Black
Plaid Gallery Glass Window Colour:
  Crystal Clear
  Cameo Ivory
  Amber
  Blue Diamond
  Sunny Yellow
  Ruby Red
Toothpicks
Pin

METHOD

Remove glass from frame to decorate and place design underneath.

Use Liquid Leading to outline the design and set aside to dry for approximately 12 to 24 hours.

When piping the mouth in leading, use a pin to pull the wet leading to a finer line.

Refer to design for colour placement. Work each outlined section individually, and apply Window Colour in the following sequence:

Bear Use Amber to colour all parts of the bear. Comb through paint with a toothpick to distribute the paint colour evenly.

Use Cameo Ivory for the nose section and feet.

Ribbon Paint with Ruby Red

Bikini Paint with Blue Diamond and comb through to distribute paint. Allow to dry before using Ruby Red to apply dots over bikini.

Sand Paint with Sunny Yellow.

Sun Paint the semi-circle of sun with Sunny Yellow. For the outer tips of sun, apply a small amount of Ruby Red at the inner edge and blend with Sunny Yellow to create a stronger, more orange shade.

Background Apply Crystal Clear to the background areas. First apply the paint, making sure the paint touches the edge of leading. Wait approximately five minutes before using a toothpick to swirl through the wet paint. This will create an interesting, slightly mottled texture when the paint dries.

Burst any significant air bubbles with a pin and leave your work to dry in a horizontal position for 24 to 48 hours.

Paint frame in a coordinating colour, and, when dry, clip glass back into frame.

Illustration shown at actual size

DAFFODILS

Illustrated in Figure 17

MATERIALS

Frame with clip-in glass, approx. 28 x 34 cm
  (11 x 13.5 in)
Plaid Gallery Glass Liquid Leading:
  Soft Black
Plaid Gallery Glass Window Colour:
  Crystal Clear
  Sunny Yellow
  Orange Poppy
  Emerald Green
  Ivy Green
Toothpicks
Pin

METHOD

Remove glass from frame to decorate and place design underneath.

Use Liquid Leading to outline the design and set aside to dry for approximately 12 to 24 hours.

Refer to design for colour placement. Work each outlined section individually, and apply Window Colour in the following sequence:

Flowers Use Sunny Yellow to colour the upper portion of the daffodil trumpet. Comb through with a toothpick to distribute the paint evenly. For the petals and bowl of the daffodil, you will need to first apply Sunny Yellow, then a few drops of Orange Poppy to form the deeper, shaded areas. While both paints are still wet, use a toothpick to swirl the colours together, creating a deeper shade.

Stems and Leaves Refer to the design for colour placement, and apply varying greens to the leaves and stems. Comb through with a toothpick to distribute the paint and use a pin to burst any larger bubbles.

Background Apply Crystal Clear to the background areas, completing each section before beginning the next. First apply the paint, making sure the paint touches the edge of the leading. Wait approximately five minutes before using a toothpick to swirl through the wet paint. This will create an interesting, slightly mottled texture when the paint dries.

Burst any significant air bubbles with a pin and leave your work in a horizontal position for 24 to 48 hours.

Paint frame in a co-ordinating colour, and when dry, clip glass back into frame.

Illustration shown at 65% of original size

TULIPS

Illustrated in Figure 18

MATERIALS

Frame with clip-in glass, approx. 28 x 34 cm
  (11 x 13 ½ in)
Plaid Gallery Glass Liquid Leading:
  Soft Black
Plaid Gallery Glass Window Colour:
  Crystal Clear
  Sunny Yellow
  Ruby Red
  Kelly Green
  Emerald Green
Toothpicks
Pin

METHOD

Remove glass from frame to decorate and place design underneath.

Use Liquid Leading to outline the design and set aside to dry for approximately 12 to 24 hours.

Refer to design for colour placement. Work each outlined section individually, apply Window Colour in the following sequence.

Flowers Apply Ruby Red to the upper portion of longest tulip, and Sunny Yellow to the lower section. Comb through individual areas to distribute the colour and then with a toothpick, use a back and forth motion to slightly streak the colours together. Reverse the colour placement for the shorter tulip and follow the same method for applying the paint.

Stems and Leaves Refer to the design for colour placement and apply varying greens to the leaves and stems. Comb through with a toothpick to distribute the paint and use a pin to burst any larger bubbles.

Background Apply Crystal Clear to the background areas, completing each section at a time. First apply the paint, making sure the paint touches the edge of the leading. Wait approximately five minutes before using a toothpick to swirl through the wet paint. This will create an interesting, slightly mottled texture when the paint dries.

Burst any significant air bubbles with a pin and leave your work in a horizontal position for 24 to 48 hours.

Paint frame in a coordinating colour, and when dry, clip glass back into frame.

Illustration shown at 65% of original size

KISSING FISH

Illustrated in Figure 19
MATERIALS
Frame with clip-in glass, approx.
  30.5 x 20 cm (12 x 8 in)
Plaid Gallery Glass Liquid Leading:
  Soft Black
Plaid Gallery Glass Window Colour:
  Crystal Clear
  Snow White
  Lime Green
  Emerald Green
  Turquoise
  Blue Diamond
  Amethyst
Toothpicks
Pin

METHOD
Remove glass from frame to decorate and place design underneath.

Use Liquid Leading to outline the design and set aside to dry for approximately 12 to 24 hours. Liquid Leading is also used for the centre of the fish eye. Use a pin to swirl through wet leading to enlarge circle.

Refer to design for colour placement. Work each outlined section individually, apply Window Colour in the following sequence.

Left Fish Use Lime Green to colour the body of the fish (except stripes). Comb through wet paint with a toothpick to distribute paint evenly.
Fins/Stripes Paint with Blue Diamond.
Tail For main tail area, use Emerald Green and then Blue Diamond for the stripe on tail.
Lips Paint with Emerald Green.

Eye The outer rim of the eye is painted with Snow White.

Right Fish Use Blue Diamond to paint the main body of the fish (except for the gills, which are painted in Turquoise).
Fins Paint with Lime Green.
Tail For main tail area, use Blue Diamond and then Lime Green for the stripe on tail.
Lips Paint with Turquoise.
Eye The outer rim of the eye is painted with Snow White.

Bubbles Paint with Snow White.
Background Apply Crystal Clear to the main background area. First apply the paint, making sure the paint touches the edge of the leading. Wait approximately five minutes before using a toothpick to swirl through the wet paint. This will create an interesting, slightly mottled texture when the Crystal Clear paint dries.
Border Use Amethyst to paint the inner section of border, and Turquoise for the outer section.

Burst any larger air-bubbles with a pin and leave your work to dry in a horizontal position for 24 to 48 hours.

Paint frame in a coordinating colour, and when dry, clip glass back into frame.

Illustration shown at 80% of original size

CATS

Illustrated in Figure 20

MATERIALS

Frame with clip-in glass, approx. 25 x 20 cm
  (9 ¾ x 8 in)
Plaid Gallery Glass Liquid Leading:
  Soft Black
Plaid Gallery Glass Window Colour:
  Crystal Clear
  White Pearl
  Hot Pink
  Denim Blue
Toothpicks
Pin

METHOD

Remove glass from frame to decorate and place design underneath.

Use Liquid Leading to outline the design and set aside to dry for approximately 12 to 24 hours. Note: To pipe the whiskers and face details, you will find it much easier to make the nozzle finer by using the sticky tape method (discussed in the Hints section of book on page 6).

Refer to design for colour placement. Work each outlined section individually, apply Window Colour in the following sequence:

Blue Cat Use Denim Blue to paint all of the cat except for the tail and neck contrast. Comb through with a toothpick to distribute the paint evenly. Use White Pearl for the remaining areas and comb through with a toothpick.

Burst any larger bubbles with a pin.

Pink Cat Use Hot Pink to paint all of the cat except for the body contrast areas. Comb through with a toothpick to distribute the paint evenly. Use White Pearl for the remaining areas and comb through with a toothpick.

Background Apply Crystal Clear to the main background area. First apply the paint, making sure the paint touches the edge of the leading. Wait approximately five minutes before using a toothpick to swirl through the wet paint. This will create an interesting, slightly mottled texture when the Crystal Clear paint dries.

Burst any significant air bubbles with a pin and leave your work to dry in a horizontal position for 24 to 48 hours. When dry, clip back into frame.

Frame I have painted a coordinating frame for this simple design. Basecoat in the colour of your choice and when dry, lightly mark the triangle shape with pencil. Over the top of pencil lines, use a dimensional fabric paint to border off each section. When dry, paint the triangles with contrast colours. Once the paint has dried, you can squeeze beads of dimensional fabric paint at random over some of the triangular shapes.

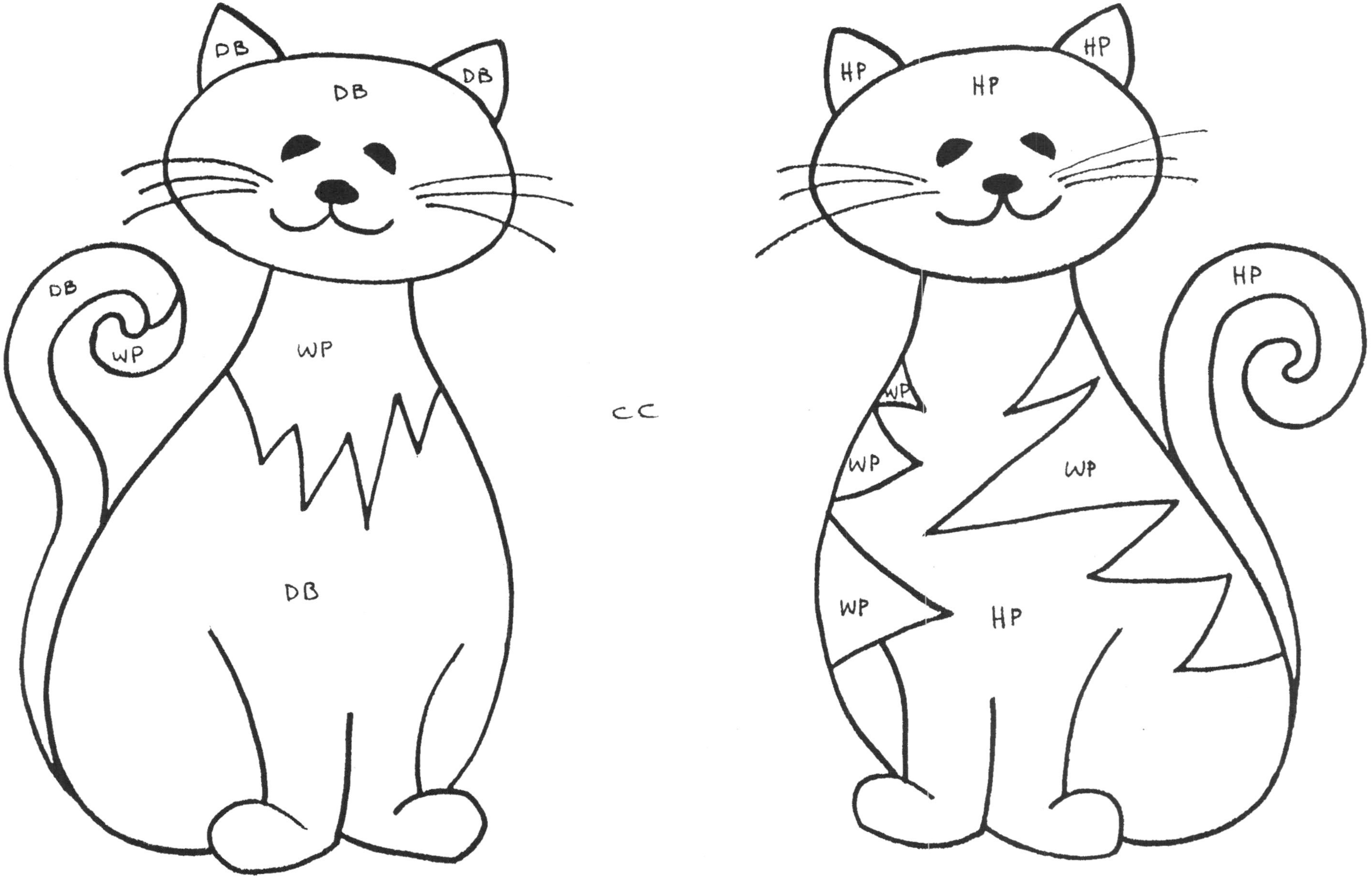

Illustration shown at actual size

TEAPOT AND CUPS

Illustrated in Figure 21

MATERIALS

Frame with clip-in glass, approx. 51 x 20 cm
 (20 x 8 in)
Plaid Gallery Glass Liquid Leading:
 Soft Black
Plaid Gallery Glass Window Colour:
 Crystal Clear
 Snow White
 White Pearl
 Cameo Ivory
 Sunny Yellow
 Amber
 Blue Diamond
 Royal Blue
Toothpicks
Pin

METHOD

Remove glass from frame to decorate and place design underneath.

Use Liquid Leading to outline the design. Set aside to dry for approximately 12 to 24 hours.

Refer to design for colour placement. Work each outlined section individually and apply Window Colour in the following sequence.

Teapot Paint the teapot with Blue Diamond, completing each outlined section before beginning the text. Comb through wet paint with a toothpick to distribute paint evenly. Allow Blue Diamond paint to dry before squeezing large dots of Sunny Yellow around middle section of teapot.

Teacups Use Sunny Yellow to paint both teacups and allow this paint to dry before squeezing small dots of Blue Diamond over cups to decorate.

Cakes Use Cameo Ivory to paint the icing and Amber for the decoration on top of each cake. The base of each cake is painted with White Pearl.

Plate Paint with Blue Diamond and comb through wet paint to distribute evenly.

Tablecoth Use Snow White to paint the main area of the cloth, combing through at intervals to distribute the paint evenly. The lace on the edge of cloth is painted in White Pearl.

Underneath cloth Paint with Royal Blue and comb through wet paint with a toothpick.

Background Apply Crystal Clear to the background area. First apply the paint, making sure the paint touches the edge of the leading. Wait approximately five minutes before using a toothpick to swirl through the wet paint. This will create an interesting, slightly mottled texture when the Crystal Clear paint dries.

Use a pin to burst any larger air bubbles and then leave your work to dry in a horizontal position for 24 to 48 hours to dry.

Paint frame in a coordinating colour and when dry, clip glass back into frame.

Illustration shown at 50% of original size

LEMON TOPIARY TREE

Illustrated in Figure 22

MATERIALS

Frame with clip-in glass, approx.
  27.5 x 34 cm (11¾ x 13½ in)
Plaid Gallery Glass Liquid Leading:
  Soft Black
Plaid Gallery Glass Window Colour:
  Crystal Clear
  Sunny Yellow
  Citrus Yellow
  Gold Sparkle
  Cocoa Brown
  Kelly Green
  Ivy Green
Toothpicks
Pin

METHOD

Remove glass from frame to decorate and place design underneath. Use Liquid Leading to outline the design.

  Note: A pin can be used to pull the wet leading into a more definite point at the tip of each lemon. Set aside to dry for approximately 12 to 24 hours.

Refer to design for colour placement. Work each outlined section individually, apply Window Colour in the following sequence:

Lemons Alternate between Citrus Yellow and Sunny Yellow to colour the lemons. Refer to design for the correct colour placement.

Tree Apply Kelly Green and Ivy Green to different areas of the background foliage, and while both paints are still wet, comb through to slightly blend the two greens together.

Trunk Use Cocoa Brown

Pot Apply Gold Sparkle to all areas of the pot and comb through to distribute the paint evenly. Allow this base colour to dry before squeezing Citrus Yellow dots over the lattice detail.

Background Apply Crystal Clear to the background area. First apply the paint, making sure the paint touches the edge of the leading. Wait approximately five minutes before using a toothpick to swirl through the wet paint. This will create an interesting, slightly mottled texture when the Crystal Clear paint dries.

Yellow Border Use Citrus Yellow to paint the border.

  Burst any larger air bubbles with a pin and leave your work to dry in a horizontal position for 24 to 48 hours.

Paint frame in a coordinating colour, and when dry, clip glass back into frame.

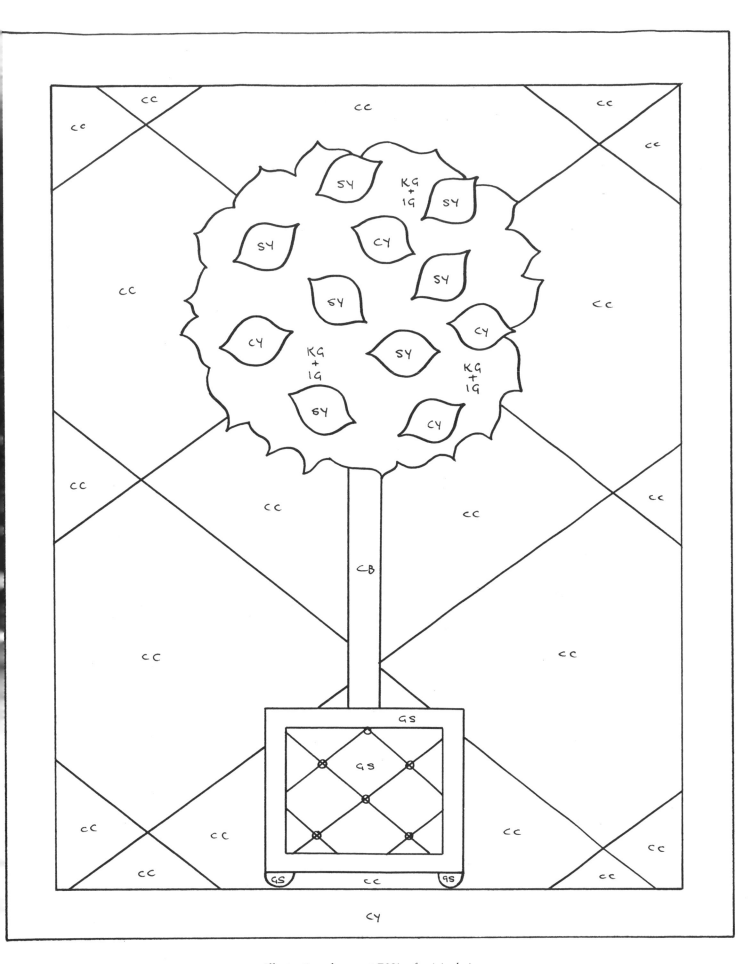

Illustration shown at 70% of original size

PEEL AND PRESS DESIGNS

Here are some smaller, fun designs that can be worked onto A4 plastic sleeves. When dry, these can be peeled off the plastic and adhered to windows or tiles.

To position, clean the glass surface to make sure it is free of any grease or dust. Press the 'peel and press' design firmly onto the glass surface, pushing any air out from underneath with your fingertips.

They can be re-positioned several times, but will gradually loose their gripping ability if re-positioned too often.

Remember, any of the designs in this book can also be used individually in this way, rather than in the framed art.

BEES

Illustrated in Figure 32
(See page 43 for template)
MATERIALS
Plaid Gallery Glass Liquid Leading:
  Soft Black
Plaid Gallery Glass Window Colour
  Black Onyx
  Citrus Yellow
  White Pearl
Plastic A4 sleeve
Toothpicks
Pin

METHOD
Note: For these smaller designs, you may find it easier to make the nozzle finer by following the directions mentioned in the Hints section on page 6.

Insert design inside the plastic sleeve and outline with Liquid Leading. Allow to dry for 12 to 24 hours or until the leading is firm.

Apply Window Colour in the following sequence.

Body Paint the first and third stripe on each bee, in Citrus Yellow. Paint remaining stripes in Black Onyx. Comb through with a toothpick to distribute the paint.

Wings Use White Pearl to paint the wings on both bees, comb through with a toothpick to distribute paint.

Burst any larger bubbles with a pin and allow to dry for 24 to 48 hours. When completely dry, gently peel the design off the plastic and attach it to a clean glass or tile surface, pressing firmly from the top downwards to remove any air bubbles. It will remain quite firmly attached to this surface if left undisturbed.

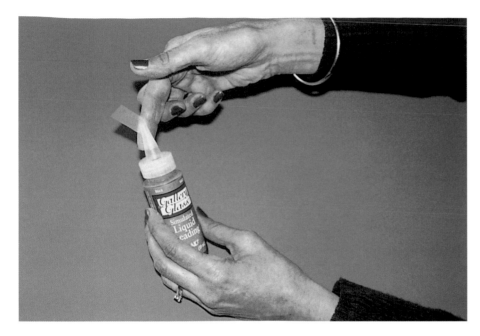

Figure 1: Prepare liquid leading bottle

Figure 2: Outlining the design on A4 plastic sleeve

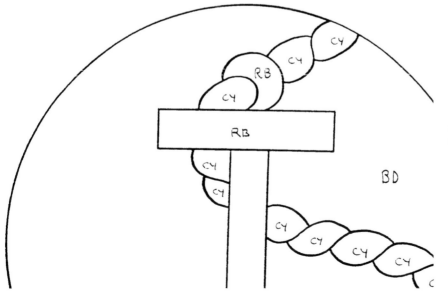

Figure 3: Pull smaller leading detail into shape with a pin

FIGURE 4: *Mixing paint colours with a toothpick*

FIGURE 5: *Adding dimensional paint detail*

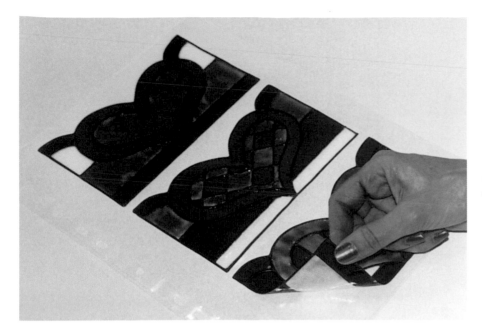

FIGURE 6: *Peel the dried design element off plastic backing*

FIGURE 7: *Carefully attach to clean glass surface and press firmly in place*

FIGURE 8: *Decorated Coffee Jars (see pages 12–16)*

FIGURE 9: *Alternatively – pipe directly onto glass coffee jars by placing design inside jar, then steady with books*

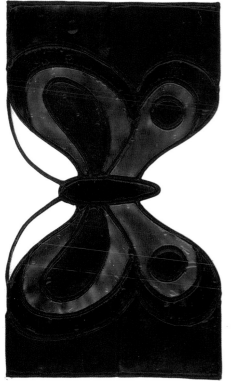

FIGURE 11: *Butterflies (see pages 16–17)*

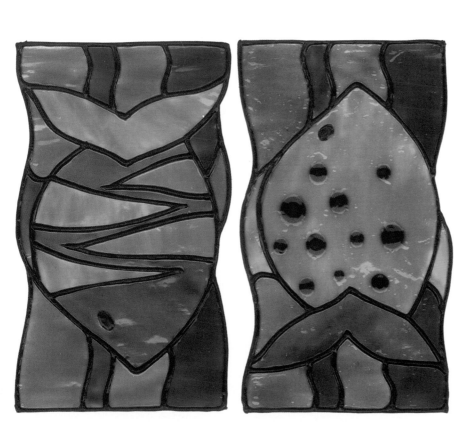
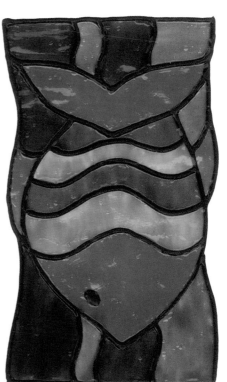
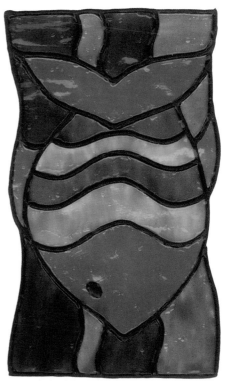

FIGURE 10: *Fish (see pages 14–1.5)*

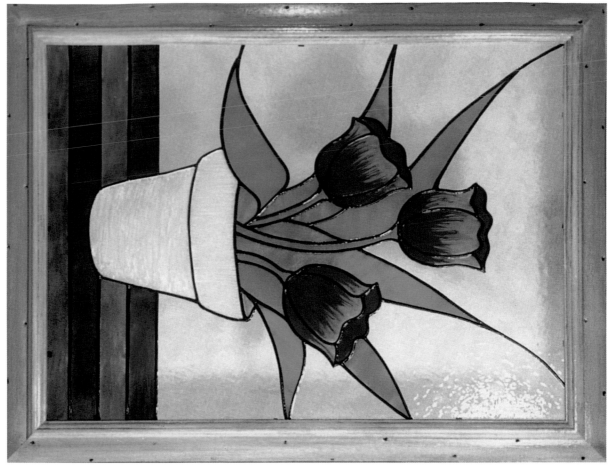

FIGURE 12: *Tulips in Pot (see pages 18–19)*

FIGURE 13: *Cinerarias in Pot (see pages 20–21)*

FIGURE 14: *Peacock (see pages 22–23)*

FIGURE 15: *Bear on Swing (see pages 24–25)*

FIGURE 16: *Bear in Bikini (see pages 26–27)*

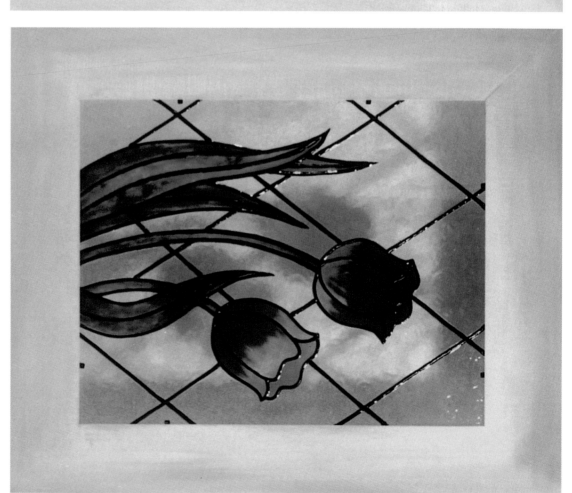

FIGURE 17: *Daffodils (see pages 28–29)*

FIGURE 18: *Tulips (see pages 30–31)*

FIGURE 19: *Kissing Fish (see pages 32–33)*

FIGURE 20: *Cats (see pages 34–35)*

FIGURE 21: *Teapot and Cups (see pages 36–37)*

FIGURE 22: *Lemon Topiary Tree (see pages 38–39)*

FIGURE 23: *Blue Yacht (see pages 60–61)*   FIGURE 24: *Yellow Yacht (see pages 62–63)*

FIGURE 25: *Anchor (see pages 64–65)*   FIGURE 26: *Life Ring (see pages 66–67)*

FIGURE 27: *Mobiles shown hanging*

FIGURE 30: Mauve Fairy
(see pages 48–49)

FIGURE 28:
Pink Fairy
(see pages 44–45)

FIGURE 29:
Blue Fairy
(see pages 46–47)

FIGURE 31: Green Fairy
(see pages 50–51)

FIGURE 32: *Bees/Daisies/Caterpillar (see pages 40–43)*

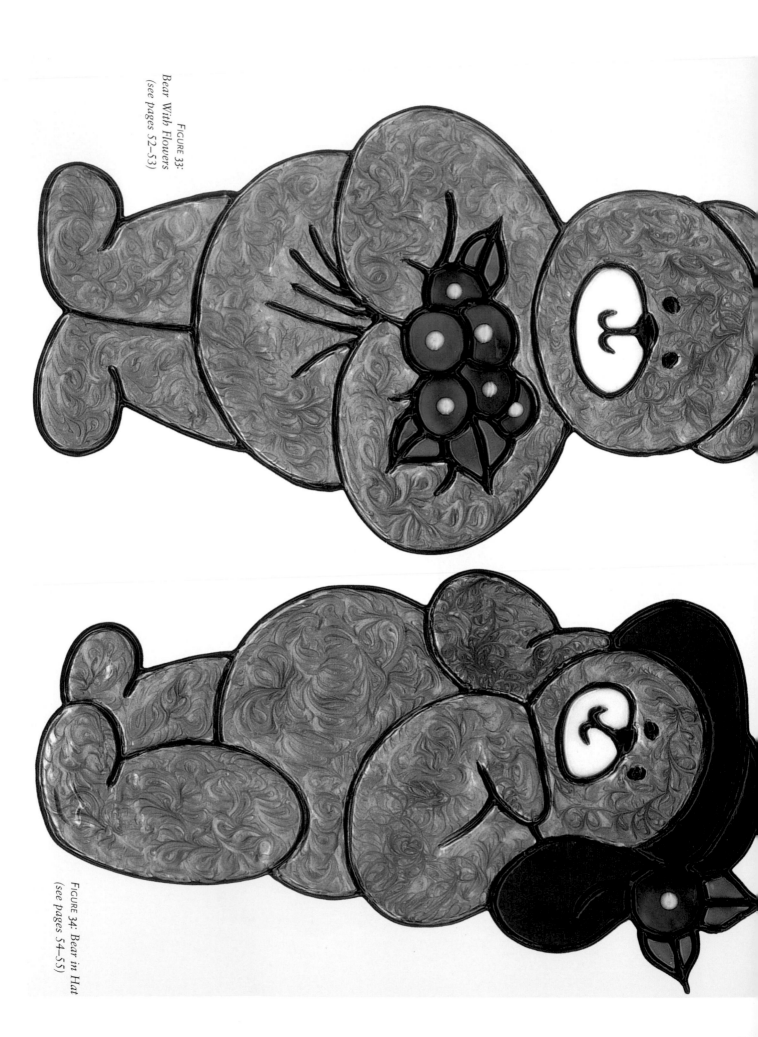

FIGURE 33:
Bear With Flowers
(see pages 52–53)

FIGURE 34: Bear in Hat
(see pages 54–55)

FIGURE 35: *Sitting Frog (see pages 56–57)*

FIGURE 36: *Peeping Frog (see pages 58–59)*

DAISIES

Illustrated in Figure 32

(See page 43 for template)

MATERIALS

Plaid Gallery Glass Liquid Leading:
  Soft Black
Plaid Gallery Glass Window Colour:
  Citrus Yellow
  Blue Diamond
  Royal Blue
  Lime Green
  Magenta Royale
  Hot Pink
  Emerald Green
Plastic A4 sleeve
Toothpicks
Pin

METHOD

Note: For these smaller designs, you may find it easier to make the nozzle finer, by following the directions in the Hints section on page 6.

Insert design inside the plastic sleeve and outline with Liquid Leading. Allow to dry for 12 to 24 hours or until the leading is firm.

Apply Window Colour in the following sequence:

Flower Centres Use Citrus Yellow to colour both centres.

Blue Daisy Apply Royal Blue to the inside area of each petal and Blue Diamond to outer edges. While both paints are wet, use a toothpick in a back and forth motion to streak the colours together slightly.

Stem/Leaves Paint with Lime Green.

Pink Daisy Apply Magenta Royale to the inside area of each petal and Hot Pink to outer edges. While both paints are wet, use a toothpick in a back and forth motion to streak the colours together slightly.

Stem/Leaves Paint with Emerald Green.

Burst any larger bubbles with a pin and allow to dry for 24 to 48 hours. When completely dry, gently peel the design off the plastic and attach it to a clean glass or tile surface, pressing firmly from the top downwards to remove any air bubbles. It will remain quite firmly attached to this surface if left undisturbed.

CATERPILLAR

MATERIALS

Plaid Gallery Glass Liquid Leading:
  Soft Black
Plaid Gallery Glass Window Colour:
  Sunny Yellow
  Lime Green
Plaid Dimensional Fabric Paint
  Deep Purple Pearl
  Bright Pink Shiny
Plastic A4 sleeve
Toothpicks
Pin

METHOD

Note: for these smaller designs, you may find it easier to make the nozzle finer, by following the directions in the Hints section.

Insert design inside the plastic sleeve and outline with Liquid Leading. Allow to dry for 12 to 24 hours or until the leading is firm to the touch.

Apply Window Colour in the following sequence:

Body Apply Sunny Yellow to the top of the body and Lime Green to the remainder of caterpillar. While both paints are still wet, use a toothpick to swirl the colours together slightly. Allow to dry before squeezing dots of pink and purple fabric paint along the upper body section.

Burst any larger bubbles with a pin and allow to dry for 24 to 48 hours. When completely dry, gently peel the design off the plastic and attach it to a clean glass or tile surface, pressing firmly from the top downwards to remove any air bubbles. It will remain quite firmly attached to this surface if left undisturbed.

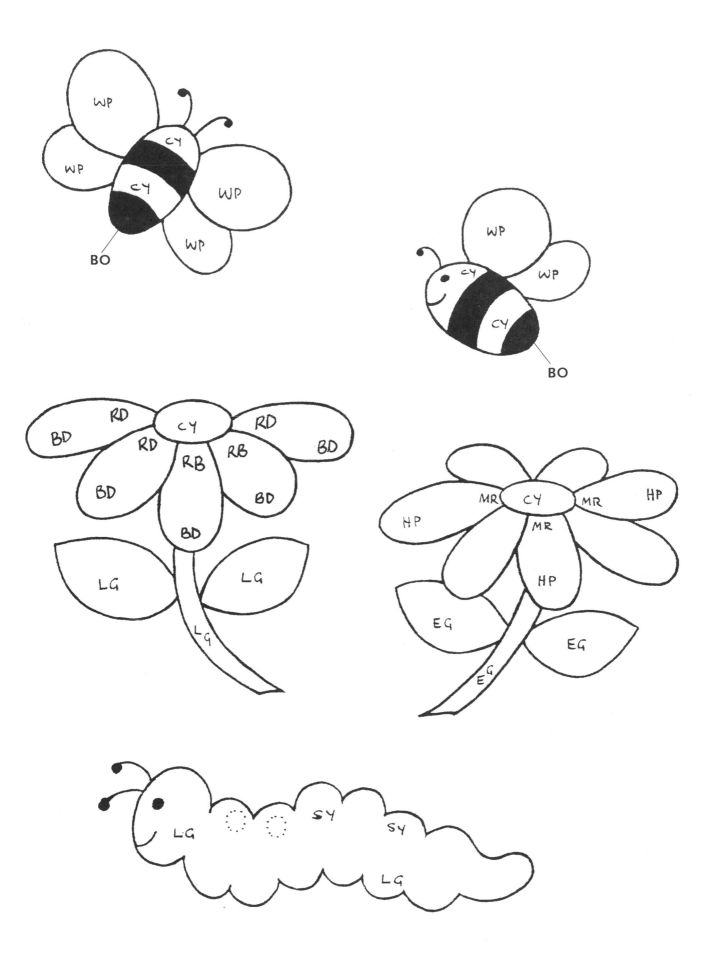

Illustration shown at actual size

PINK FAIRY

Illustrated in Figure 28

MATERIALS

Plaid Gallery Glass Liquid Leading:
  Soft Black
Plaid Gallery Glass Window Colour:
  White Pearl
  Gold sparkle
  Sunny yellow
  Canyon Coral
  Hot Pink
  Magenta Royale
  Berry Red
Plastic A4 sleeve
Toothpicks
Pin

METHOD

Insert design inside the plastic sleeve and outline with Liquid Leading. Allow to dry for 12 to 24 hours or until the leading is firm to the touch.

The mouth is created in Liquid Leading by squeezing a small dot of leading, then while leading is still wet, pulling out both corners with a pin. This is an easier way to create a much finer finish on the mouth.

Apply Window Colour in the following sequence:

Body Use Canyon Coral to colour all areas of body, and comb through with a toothpick to make colour even.

Cheeks Apply Canyon Coral to all of face area and use a toothpick to carefully push paint around face details. Be sure the paint touches all areas of leading. Comb through with a toothpick to make colour even. Pick up a tiny amount of Magenta Royale on the tip of a pin and while Canyon Coral is still wet, swirl Magenta Royale around in a circle to create rosy cheeks.

Hair Use Sunny Yellow in all hair sections.

Top Colour with Hot pink and comb through to distribute paint evenly.

Skirt First apply Berry Red to the upper portion of skirt and comb through with a toothpick. Then to the lower skirt area apply Magenta Royale and comb through. Now while both paints are still wet, use a toothpick in a back and forth motion to streak colours together slightly.

Shoes Colour with Berry Red.

Wing Apply White Pearl to wings and comb through with a toothpick. While paint is still wet, squeeze a dot of Magenta Royale, then swirl in a small circle with a toothpick.

Wand Colour with Gold Sparkle and comb through with a toothpick to make colour even.

Burst any larger bubbles with a pin and allow to dry for 24 to 48 hours. When completely dry, gently peel the design off the plastic and attach it to a clean glass or tile surface, pressing firmly from the top downwards to remove any air bubbles. It will remain quite firmly attached to this surface if left undisturbed.

Illustration shown at actual size

BLUE FAIRY

Illustrated in Figure 29

MATERIALS

Plaid Gallery Glass Liquid Leading:
  Soft Black
Plaid Gallery Glass Window Colour:
  Canyon Coral
  Magenta Royale
  Amber
  Blue Diamond
  Royal Blue
  Sunny Yellow
  White Pearl
Plastic A4 sleeve
Toothpicks
Pin

METHOD

Insert design inside the plastic sleeve and outline with Liquid Leading.

Allow to dry for 12 to 24 hours or until the leading is firm to the touch.

The mouth is created by first squeezing a small dot of leading, then while leading is still wet, pulling out both corners with a pin. This is an easier way to create a much finer finish on the mouth.

Apply Window Colour in the following sequence:

Body Use Canyon Coral to colour all areas of body, and comb through with a toothpick to make colour even.

Cheeks Apply Canyon Coral to all of face area. Be sure the paint touches all areas of leading. Comb through with a toothpick to make colour even. Pick up a tiny amount of Magenta Royale on the tip of a pin and while Canyon Coral is still wet, swirl Magenta Royale around in a circle to create rosy cheeks.

Hair Use Amber to colour hair sections.

Top Colour with Blue Diamond and comb through to distribute paint evenly.

Skirt Apply Royal Blue to the upper area of the top skirt and comb through to distribute paint in this area. Then apply Blue Diamond to the remainder of the upper skirt and use a toothpick in a back and forth motion to streak colours together. Colour the lower skirt with Royal Blue and comb through wet paint with a toothpick to distribute the paint evenly.

Shoes Colour with Royal Blue

Wings Apply White Pearl to wings and comb through with a toothpick. While paint is still wet, squeeze three dots of Blue Diamond onto left wing, then swirl in a small circle with a toothpick.

Flowers Colour all flowers with Sunny Yellow and while paint is still wet, squeeze a dot of Magenta Royale in the centre and swirl slightly with a toothpick.

Burst any larger bubbles with a pin and allow to dry for 24 to 48 hours. When completely dry, gently peel the design off the plastic and attach it to a clean glass or tile surface, pressing firmly from the top downwards to remove any air bubbles. It will remain quite firmly attached to this surface if left undisturbed.

Illustration shown at actual size

MAUVE FAIRY

Illustrated in Figure 30

MATERIALS

Plaid Gallery Glass Liquid Leading:
  Soft Black
Plaid Gallery Glass Window Colour:
  Canyon Coral
  White Pearl
  Clear Frost
  Citrus Yellow
  Magenta Royale
  Denim Blue
  Sapphire
Plastic A4 sleeve
Toothpicks
Pin

METHOD

Insert design inside the plastic sleeve and outline with Liquid Leading.

Allow to dry for 12 to 24 hours or until the leading is firm to the touch.

The mouth is created by first squeezing a small dot of leading, then while leading is still wet, pulling out both corners with a pin. This is an easier way to create a much finer finish on the mouth.

Apply Window Colour in the following sequence.

Body Use Canyon Coral to colour all areas of body, and comb through with a toothpick to make colour even.

Cheeks Apply Canyon Coral to all of face area. Be sure the paint touches all areas of leading. Comb through with a toothpick to make colour even. Pick up a tiny amount of Magenta Royale on the tip of a pin and while Canyon Coral is still wet, swirl Magenta Royale around in a circle to create rosy cheeks.

Hair Use Citrus Yellow to colour hair sections.

Top Colour with Denim Blue and comb through to distribute paint evenly.

Skirt Apply Denim Blue to the upper area of the skirt and comb through to distribute the paint in this area. Then apply Sapphire to the remainder of skirt and use a toothpick in a back and forth motion to streak colours together.

Shoes Colour with Sapphire.

Wings Apply White Pearl to wings and comb through with a toothpick. While paint is still wet, squeeze dots of Sapphire, then swirl in a small circle with a toothpick.

Cloud Apply Clear Frost to all cloud areas but before combing through, squeeze at random small dots of White Pearl and while both paints are still wet, use a toothpick to swirl the paints to distribute more evenly. When paint has dried it will have a soft hazy effect.

Halo Colour this small area with Clear Frost and comb through to distribute paint evenly.

Burst any larger bubbles with a pin and allow to dry for 24 to 48 hours. When completely dry, gently peel the design off the plastic and attach it to a clean glass or tile surface, pressing firmly from the top downwards to remove any air bubbles. It will remain quite firmly attached to this surface if left undisturbed.

GREEN FAIRY

Illustrated in Figure 31

MATERIALS

Plaid Gallery Glass Liquid Leading:

Soft Black

Plaid Gallery Glass Window Colour:

White Pearl

Canyon Coral

Magenta Royale

Citrus Yellow

Light Brown

Kelly Green

Emerald Green

Plastic A4 sleeve

Toothpicks

Pin

METHOD

Insert design inside the plastic sleeve and outline with Liquid Leading.

Allow to dry for 12 to 24 hours or until the leading is firm to the touch.

The mouth is created by first squeezing a small dot of leading, then while leading is still wet, pulling out at both corners with a pin. This is an easy way to create a much finer finish on the mouth.

Apply Window Colour in the following sequence:

Body Use Canyon Coral to colour all areas of body, and comb through with a toothpick to make colour even.

Cheeks Apply Canyon Coral to all of face. Be sure the paint touches all areas of leading.

Comb through with a toothpick to make colour even. Pick up a tiny amount of Magenta Royale on the tip of a pin and while Canyon Coral is still wet, swirl Magenta Royale around in a circle to create rosy cheeks.

Hair Use Light Brown to colour hair sections

Top Colour with Kelly Green and comb through to distribute paint evenly.

Skirt Apply Emerald Green to the upper areas of skirt layers and comb through to distribute paint in this area. Then apply Kelly Green to the remainder of skirt layers and use a toothpick in a back and forth motion to streak colours together.

Shoes Colour with Emerald Green.

Wings Apply White Pearl to wings and comb through with a toothpick. While paint is still wet, squeeze dots of Emerald Green, then swirl in a small circle with a toothpick.

Flower Colour with Citrus Yellow and while paint is wet, squeeze a small dot of Magenta Royale in the centre of flower and swirl slightly with a toothpick.

Burst any larger bubbles with a pin and allow to dry for 24 to 48 hours. When completely dry, gently peel the design off the plastic and attach it to a clean glass or tile surface, pressing firmly from the top downwards to remove any air bubbles. It will remain quite firmly attached to this surface if left undisturbed.

Illustration shown at actual size

BEAR WITH FLOWERS

Illustrated in Figure 33

MATERIALS

Plaid Gallery Glass Liquid Leading:
  Soft Black
Plaid Gallery Glass Window Colour:
  Copper Sparkle
  Cameo Ivory
  Lime Green
  Blue Diamond
  Sunny Yellow
Plastic A4 sleeve
Toothpicks
Pin

METHOD

Insert design inside plastic sleeve and outline in Liquid Leading. A finer line on the mouth can be achieved by pulling the wet leading with a pin. Allow leading to dry 12 to 24 hours or until firm to touch.

Apply Window colour in the following sequence:

Bear Apply Copper Sparkle to the bear's face and body (except for the nose area). Comb through with a toothpick to distribute paint evenly, before using the toothpick to swirl through the wet paint to give a textured effect.

Nose Use Cameo Ivory to colour nose area and comb through with a toothpick.

Flowers Use Blue Diamond to colour each flower and comb through with a toothpick. Allow the blue paint to dry before squeezing a dot of Sunny Yellow for the centre of each flower.

Leaves Colour with Lime Green.

Burst any larger bubbles with a pin and allow to dry for 24 to 48 hours. When completely dry, gently peel the bear off the plastic and attach it to a clean glass or tile surface, pressing firmly from the top downwards to remove any air bubbles. It will remain quite firmly attached to this surface if left undisturbed.

Illustration shown at actual size

BEAR IN HAT

Illustrated in Figure 34

MATERIALS

Plaid Gallery Glass Liquid Leading:
  Soft Black
Plaid Gallery Glass Window Colour:
  Copper Sparkle
  Cameo Ivory
  Lime Green
  Magenta Royale
  Blue Diamond
  Sunny Yellow
Plastic A4 sleeve
Toothpicks
Pin

METHOD

Insert design inside plastic sleeve and outline in Liquid Leading. A finer line on the mouth can be achieved by pulling the wet leading with a pin. Allow leading to dry 12 to 24 hours or until firm to touch.

Apply Window colour in the following sequence.

Bear Apply Copper Sparkle to the bear's face and body (except for the nose area). Comb through with a toothpick to distribute paint evenly, before using the toothpick to swirl through the wet paint to give a textured effect.

Nose Use Cameo Ivory to colour nose area and comb through with a toothpick.

Hat Colour with Magenta Royale and comb through with a toothpick to distribute paint evenly.

Flower Use Blue Diamond to paint the flower. Allow blue paint to dry before squeezing a dot of Sunny Yellow for the flower centre.

Leaves Colour with Lime Green.

Burst any larger bubbles with a pin and allow to dry for 24 to 48 hours. When completely dry, gently peel the bear off the plastic and attach it to a clean glass or tile surface, pressing firmly from the top downwards to remove any air bubbles. It will remain quite firmly attached to this surface if left undisturbed.

Illustration shown at actual size

SITTING FROG

Illustrated in Figure 35

MATERIALS

Plaid Gallery Glass Liquid Leading:
 Soft Black
Plaid Gallery Glass Window Colour
 Lime Green
 Ivy Green
 Emerald Green
 Amber
Plastic A4 sleeve
Toothpicks
Pin

METHOD

Insert design inside the plastic sleeve and outline with Liquid Leading. Allow leading to dry for 12 to 24 hours.

Note When piping out the leading for eyes, you will achieve a finer result if you first pipe the outer line of eye and allow this to dry. Then pipe in the more solid eye semi-circle. As the lines are quite close together, they tend to run, unless worked separately.

Apply Window Colour in the following sequence:

Frog Use Lime Green to paint all of frog. Comb through with a toothpick to distribute paint.

Waterlily Leaf Paint with Ivy Green. Comb through with a toothpick to distribute the paint.

Bullrushes Paint with Amber and comb through to distribute the paint.

Reeds Use Emerald Green to paint the three leaves, except for the turnback on the shorter leaf. On the turnback, use a combination of Emerald and Lime Green (equal amounts). Mix two similar-sized drops of paint in the outlined area, then push to meet edge of leading with toothpick. Comb through paint to distribute evenly.

Burst any larger bubbles with a pin and allow to dry for 24 to 48 hours. When completely dry, gently peel the design off the plastic and attach it to a clean glass or tile surface, pressing firmly from the top downwards to remove any air. It will remain quite firmly attached to this surface if left undisturbed.

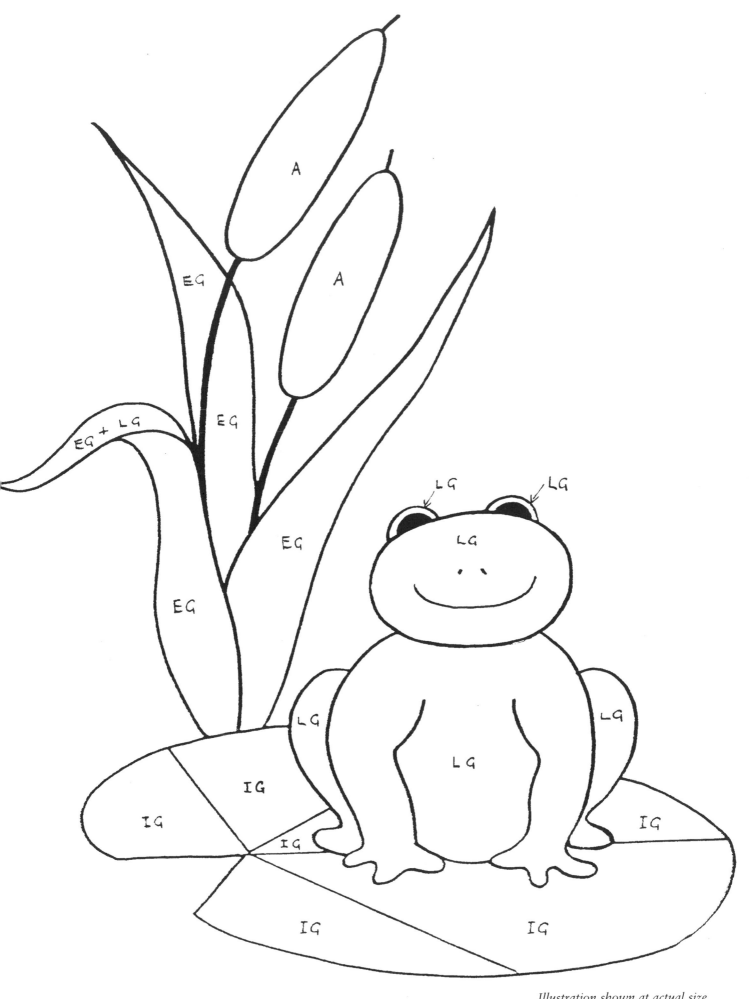

Illustration shown at actual size

PEEPING FROG

Illustrated in Figure 36

MATERIALS

Plaid Gallery Glass Liquid Leading:
  Soft Black
Plaid Gallery Glass Window Colour:
  Lime Green
  Ivy Green
  Turquoise
  White Pearl
  Magenta Royale
Plastic A4 sleeve
Toothpicks
Pin

METHOD

Insert design inside the plastic sleeve and outline with Liquid Leading.

Allow to dry for 12 to 24 hours.

Note When piping out the leading for the eyes, you will achieve a finer result if you first pipe the outer line of the eye and allow this to dry. Then pipe in the more solid eye semi-circle. As the lines are quite close together, they tend to run, unless worked separately.

Apply Window Colour in the following sequence:

Frog Use Lime Green to paint all of frog. Comb through with a toothpick to distribute paint.

Waterlily Leaf Paint with Ivy Green. Comb through with a toothpick to distribute paint.

Waterlily Paint the lower section of each petal with Magenta Royale. At the upper tips of petals, use Pearl White. While both paints are wet, use toothpick to blend colours together, then comb through to distribute the paint evenly.

Dragonfly Paint the body with Turquoise. Use White Pearl to paint the wings and comb through with a toothpick to distribute the paint.

Burst any larger bubbles with a pin and allow to dry for 24 to 48 hours. When completely dry, gently peel the design off the plastic and attach it to a clean glass or tile surface, pressing firmly from the top downwards to remove any air. It will remain quite firmly attached to this surface if left undisturbed.

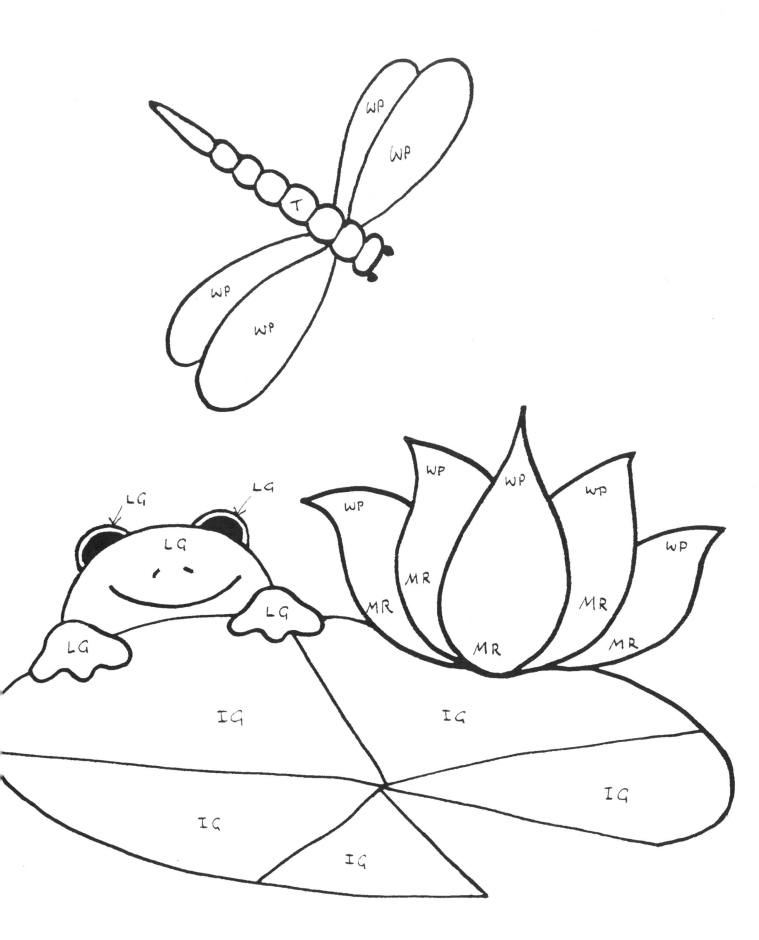

Illustration shown at actual size

MOBILES

Create a bright nautical theme in any room, by hanging these glass mobiles inside a window. You can have the glass custom cut at most glaziers and request them to drill a small hole at the top so you can hang them with fishing line.

BLUE YACHT

Illustrated in Figure 23

MATERIALS

4 mm-thick glass circle (15 cm diameter)
Plaid Gallery Glass Liquid Leading:
  Soft Black
Plaid Gallery Glass Window Colour
  Blue Diamond
  Royal Blue
  Citrus Yellow
  Sunny Yellow
  Snow White
  Blue Sparkle
Toothpicks
Pin

METHOD

Lay the round of glass over the top of the design and outline with Liquid Leading. Set aside to dry for approximately 12 to 24 hours

Apply Window Colour in the following sequence.

Sky Paint with Snow White and comb through with a toothpick to distribute paint evenly.

Striped Sail Paint the main stripes on the sail with Blue Diamond, but leave two gaps for the stripes. Allow the blue paint to dry before painting in the stripes with Sunny Yellow.

Plain Sail Paint with Royal Blue.

Hull and Flag Paint with Citrus Yellow.

Water Use Blue Sparkle to paint the water, combing through with a toothpick while paint is still wet, to distribute evenly.

Use a pin to burst any larger air bubbles and then leave your work to dry in a horizontal position for 24 to 48 hours. Tie a length of strong fishing line through the hole, and hang from window.

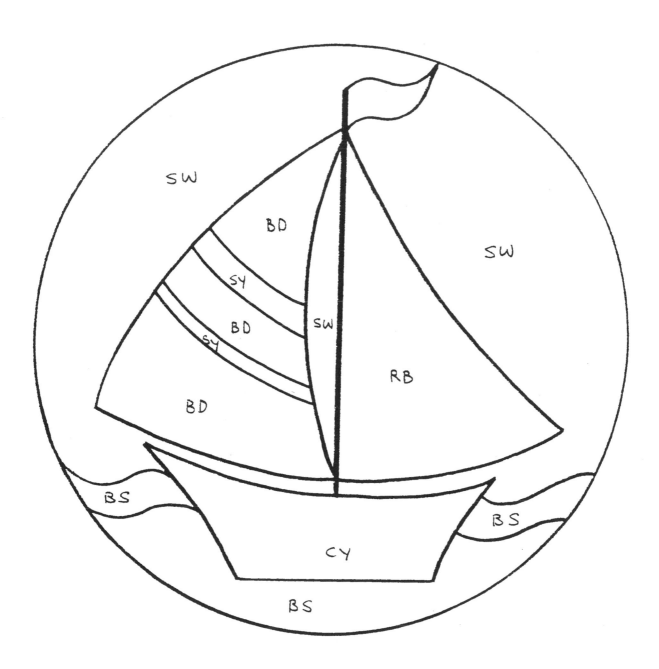

Illustration shown at actual size

YELLOW YACHT

Illustrated in Figure 24

MATERIALS

4 mm-thick glass circle (15 cm diameter)
Plaid Gallery Glass Liquid Leading:
  Soft Black
Plaid Gallery Glass Window Colour:
  Blue Diamond
  Citrus Yellow
  Sunny Yellow
  Snow White
  Blue Sparkle
Toothpicks
Pin

METHOD

Lay the round of glass over the top of the design and outline with Liquid Leading. Set aside to dry for approximately 12 to 24 hours

Apply Window Colour in the following sequence:

Sky Paint with Snow White and comb through with a toothpick to distribute paint evenly.

Spotted Sail Paint a background of Sunny Yellow and allow to dry. Use Blue Diamond to apply small dots to decorate.

Plain Sail Paint with Citrus Yellow and comb through wet paint to distribute.

Hull Paint with Blue Sparkle.

Flag and Water Paint with Blue Diamond.

Use a pin to burst any larger air bubbles and then leave your work to dry in a horizontal position for 24 to 48 hours. Tie a length of strong fishing line through the hole, and hang around window area.

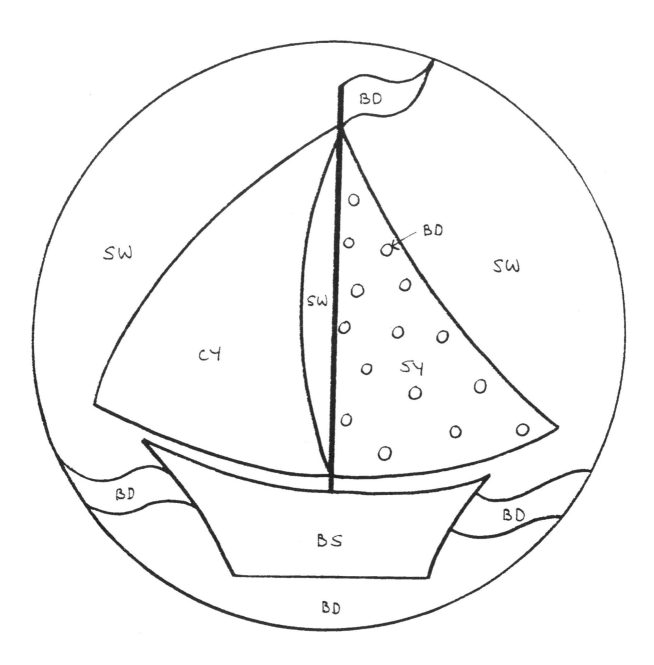

Illustration shown at actual size

ANCHOR

Illustrated in Figure 25

MATERIALS

4 mm-thick glass circle (15 cm diameter)
Plaid Gallery Glass Liquid Leading:
 Soft Black
Plaid Gallery Glass Window Colour:
 Blue Diamond
 Royal Blue
 Citrus Yellow
Toothpicks
Pin

METHOD

Lay the round of glass over the top of design and outline with Liquid Leading.

Set aside to dry for approximately 12 to 24 hours

Apply Window Colour in the following sequence.

Anchor Paint anchor with Royal Blue and comb through to distribute paint.

Rope Use Citrus Yellow to paint each section of rope.

Background Paint with Blue Diamond and comb through with a toothpick to distribute paint evenly.

Use a pin to burst any larger air bubbles and then leave your work to dry in a horizontal position for 24 to 48 hours. Tie a length of strong fishing line through hole, and hang from window area.

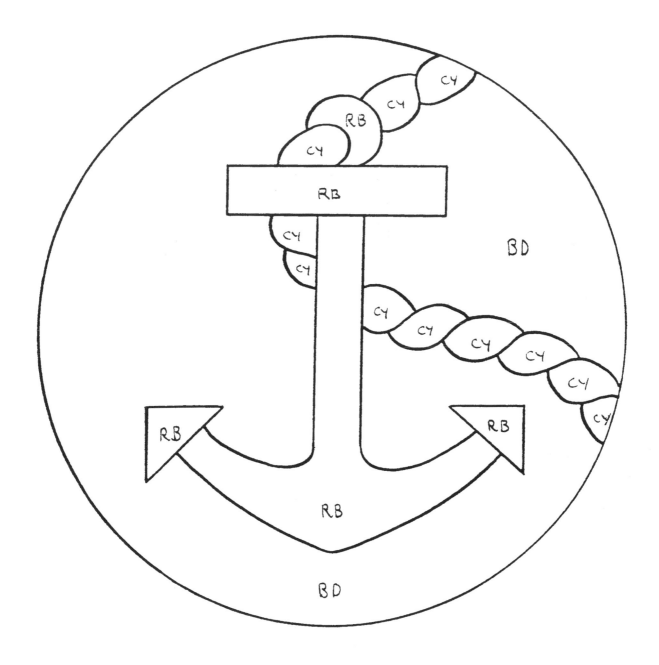

Illustration shown at actual size

LIFE RING

Illustrated in Figure 26

MATERIALS

4mm glass circle (15 cm diameter)
Plaid Gallery Glass Liquid Leading:
  Soft Black
Plaid Gallery Glass Window Colour
  Blue Diamond
  Royal Blue
  Snow White
  Sunny Yellow
Toothpicks
Pin

METHOD

Lay the round of glass over the top of the design and outline with Liquid Leading. Set aside to dry for approximately 12 to 24 hours.

Apply Window Colour in the following sequence:

Ring Paint the main area of life ring with Blue Diamond, and use Royal Blue to paint the contrasting four bands.

Rope Paint with Snow White.

Background Paint with Sunny Yellow and comb through with a toothpick to distribute paint evenly.

Use a pin to burst any larger air bubbles and then leave your work in a horizontal position for 24 to 48 hours to dry. Tie a length of strong fishing line through the hole, and hang from window area.

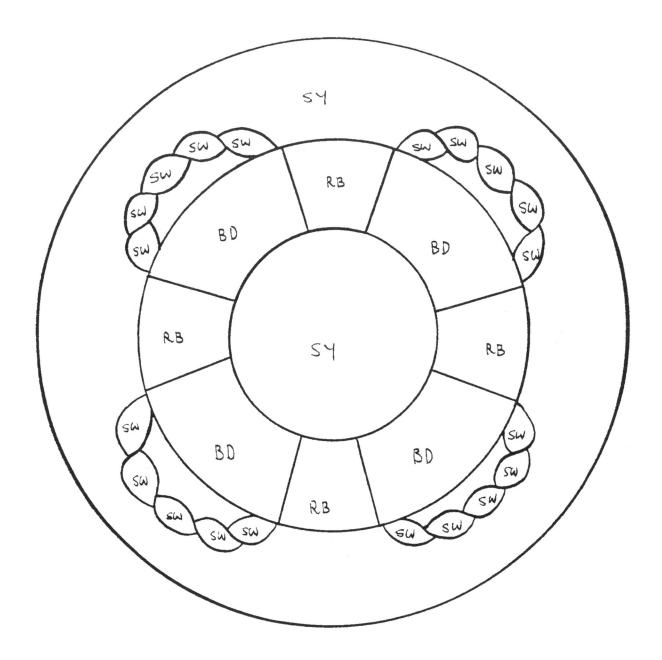

Illustration shown at actual size

INDEX

NOTES

NOTES